DIABETIC RENAL DIET SLOW COOKER COOKBOOK

Teresa Ballard

Disclaimer:

The information provided in this book is for general informational purposes only. While every effort has been made to ensure that the content is accurate and up-to-date, the author and the publisher make no representations or warranties of any kind, express or implied, about the completeness, accuracy, reliability, suitability, or availability of the information contained within these pages. Any reliance you place on such information is strictly at your own risk.

OTHER BOOKS BY THE AUTHOR

Low Potassium Slow Cooker Cookbook

Low Potassium Instant Pot Cookbook

Low Potassium Air Fryer Cookbook

Low Potassium Cookbook for Seniors

Vegetarian Low potassium Cookbook

Vegan Low Potassium Cookbook

Low Sodium Slow Cooker cookbook

Low Sodium Instant Pot Cookbook

Low Sodium Air Fryer Cookbook

Low Sodium Cookbook for Congestive Heart Failure

Low Sodium Cookbook for Kidney Disease

Low Sodium Cookbook for Beginners

Vegetarian Low Sodium Cookbook

Vegan Low Sodium Cookbook

Low Sodium Cookbook for Seniors

Low Potassium cookbook for Beginners

SCAN THE QR CODE BELOW TO SEE
MORE BOOKS BY THE AUTHOR

TABLE OF CONTENTS

INTRODUCTION

In the quiet corners of Mrs. Morgan's kitchen, where the aroma of simmering stews and the gentle hum of a slow cooker blended seamlessly, a culinary journey unfolded—a journey that transcended mere recipes and delved into the very essence of health and nourishment. Welcome to the world of the "Slow Cooker Diabetic Renal Diet Cookbook," where the sizzle of sautéed onions and the magic of carefully chosen ingredients intertwine to tell a tale of resilience, healing, and the transformative power of food.

As an experienced nutritionist, I have witnessed countless stories of triumph and transformation. Yet, none have left an indelible mark quite like Mrs. Morgan's poignant journey. A cozy kitchen, bathed in the soft glow of afternoon sunlight, where Mrs. Morgan, a spirited soul navigating the labyrinth of diabetes and renal health, found solace and strength in the rhythmic whirr of her trusty slow cooker.

It all began with a simple yet profound question: How can one embark on a culinary adventure that not only tantalizes the taste buds but also aligns seamlessly with the intricate dance of diabetes and renal wellness? The answer unfolded through the pages of the "Slow Cooker Diabetic Renal Diet Cookbook," a beacon of hope that I presented to Mrs. Morgan during one of our heartfelt conversations.

"Mrs. Morgan," I remember saying, "food is not just sustenance; it's a celebration of life. And with the right ingredients, cooked with love and patience, we can craft a symphony of flavors that not only delights the palate but also supports your health journey."

Her eyes, filled with a mixture of hope and skepticism, mirrored the countless individuals I had encountered on this journey. The world of dietary restrictions and health-conscious cooking can seem like a maze—one where joy and flavor often take a back seat to the rigidity of nutritional guidelines. However, within the pages of this cookbook lies a roadmap, a compass that guides you through the intricate terrain of diabetes and renal health.

As the velvety aroma of a slow-cooked broth wafted through Mrs. Morgan's kitchen, I saw a spark ignite within her. It was a spark that whispered of possibilities, of a life not constrained by the shackles of dietary restrictions but one that reveled in the joy of culinary creativity.

In the following weeks, our conversations became a canvas on which Mrs. Morgan painted her culinary aspirations. We discussed the subtleties of ingredient combinations, the art of slow cooking, and the harmony of flavors that would not only tickle her taste buds but also nourish her body from within.

The cookbook became her trusted companion, a worn and well-loved guide that unfolded a tapestry of recipes, each page telling a story of vitality and resilience. Mrs. Morgan's kitchen metamorphosed into a haven of healing, where the clinking of utensils became a rhythmic dance of wellness.

As the savory aromas lingered in the air, so did the sense of empowerment that permeated Mrs. Morgan's culinary endeavors. She found joy in crafting dishes that not only suited her dietary needs but also spoke to her soul. The "Slow Cooker Diabetic Renal Diet Cookbook" became more than a collection of recipes; it became a lifeline, a bridge between restriction and liberation.

In the midst of our culinary escapades, Mrs. Morgan confided in me about the newfound zest for life she discovered through the simple act of slow cooking. She shared stories of family gatherings where the rich aroma of a carefully prepared stew sparked conversations and laughter. Her eyes, once clouded with uncertainty, now sparkled with vitality, mirroring the transformation that unfolded within her kitchen and resonated throughout her entire being.

This cookbook is not just a compendium of recipes; it is a narrative of empowerment, a saga of reclaiming control over one's health and embracing the joy that food can bring. Within its pages, you will find not only delicious and wholesome recipes but also the essence of Mrs. Morgan's journey—a journey that speaks to the human spirit's ability to rise above challenges and create a symphony of health and happiness.

As you embark on this culinary odyssey with the "Slow Cooker Diabetic Renal Diet Cookbook," envision the sizzle of onions, the melody of spices, and the warmth of a slow-cooked embrace. Let Mrs. Morgan's story be the catalyst that propels you into a world where food is not just sustenance but a celebration—a celebration of life, health, and the boundless possibilities that await within the kitchen. Turn the page, and let the journey begin.

CHAPTER ONE: SLOW COOKING FOR HEALTH

Benefits of Slow Cooking for Diabetic Renal Patients

Precision in Cooking Times

One of the key advantages of slow cooking for individuals with diabetes and renal concerns is the precise control it offers over cooking times. Slow cookers operate at low temperatures over an extended period, allowing for thorough cooking without compromising the nutritional value of ingredients. This method helps in preserving essential nutrients, ensuring a health-conscious approach to meal preparation.

Blood Sugar Management

For diabetic renal patients, maintaining stable blood sugar levels is paramount. Slow cooking promotes the gradual breakdown of carbohydrates, preventing rapid spikes in blood sugar. This measured approach to digestion can aid in better glucose control, providing a gentler impact on insulin levels and reducing the risk of complications associated with diabetes.

Reduced Sodium Intake

Controlling sodium intake is crucial for individuals with renal concerns. Slow cooking allows for the use of natural flavors and herbs, reducing the need for excessive salt. This culinary technique enhances the taste of dishes while minimizing the risk of exacerbating kidney-related issues, a common concern for those with diabetes and renal conditions.

Retention of Nutrients

Slow cooking preserves the nutritional content of ingredients, ensuring that essential vitamins and minerals are retained during the cooking process. This is especially beneficial for diabetic renal patients who need a well-balanced diet to support overall health. The method's slow and steady approach prevents nutrient loss, contributing to the creation of meals that are not only flavorful but also highly nutritious.

Tenderization of Lean Proteins

For individuals with renal issues, incorporating lean proteins is essential. Slow cooking is ideal for tenderizing tougher cuts of meat without the need for excessive fats or salts. This gentle cooking process ensures that proteins remain succulent and easy to digest, catering to the dietary requirements of diabetic renal patients while maintaining a focus on health-conscious eating.

Choosing the Right Ingredients

Emphasizing Fresh and Whole Foods

The foundation of a slow cooker diabetic renal diet lies in the selection of high-quality, fresh, and whole ingredients. Opting for fresh vegetables, lean proteins, and whole grains ensures that the meals are nutrient-dense and aligned with the dietary needs of individuals managing diabetes and renal health.

Mindful Carbohydrate Choices

Carbohydrate selection plays a vital role in controlling blood sugar levels.

Whole grains, legumes, and vegetables with low glycemic indexes are excellent choices for slow cooker recipes. These options provide sustained energy and help in stabilizing blood sugar, making them suitable for those with diabetes.

Limiting Processed Ingredients

Processed foods often contain additives, preservatives, and excess sodium, which can be detrimental to renal health. Choosing fresh, unprocessed ingredients for slow cooker recipes helps in minimizing the intake of harmful substances, supporting a healthier diet for individuals managing diabetes and renal concerns.

Incorporating Kidney-Friendly Herbs and Spices

Herbs and spices not only enhance the flavor of slow-cooked meals but also offer additional health benefits. Some herbs, such as parsley and cilantro, are known for their potential kidney-cleansing properties. By incorporating these kidney-friendly herbs and spices, the slow cooker diabetic renal diet becomes a flavorful and health-promoting culinary experience.

CHAPTER TWO: ESSENTIAL GUIDELINES FOR DIABETIC RENAL DIET

Welcome to the heart of your journey towards a healthier lifestyle – Chapter Two of our Slow Cooker Diabetic Renal Diet Cookbook. Here, we delve into the essential guidelines that will serve as your compass in navigating the intricate terrain of managing both diabetes and renal health. By understanding and embracing these guidelines, you empower yourself to make informed choices that promote well-being, balance, and flavor in your culinary pursuits.

Managing Carbohydrates and Sugars

Understanding the Carbohydrate Conundrum:

Carbohydrates play a pivotal role in managing blood glucose levels. However, not all carbs are created equal. Focus on incorporating complex carbohydrates such as whole grains, legumes, and vegetables, as they provide sustained energy without causing rapid spikes in blood sugar. Opt for high-fiber options to promote digestive health and control blood sugar levels effectively.

Mindful Sweetening:

While the allure of sweetness is undeniable, it's crucial to be discerning in your choices. Replace refined sugars with natural sweeteners like stevia or monk fruit. Experiment with fruit-based sweeteners to add a burst of flavor without compromising on your health goals. Portion control is key, ensuring that your culinary creations remain both indulgent and diabetes-friendly.

Balancing Act:

Strike a harmonious balance between carbohydrates, proteins, and fats in your meals. The right combination can help regulate blood sugar levels and stave off hunger, promoting an overall sense of satisfaction. Remember, it's not about restriction but about making wise choices that align with your health objectives.

Controlling Sodium Intake

Cracking the Sodium Code:

For those navigating the intricate waters of diabetic renal health, sodium control is paramount. Excessive sodium intake can exacerbate hypertension and contribute to kidney complications. Embrace fresh, whole foods and herbs to season your dishes, reducing the need for salt. Experiment with flavorful spices to enhance taste without compromising on your health goals.

Reading Labels with Precision:

Become an astute label reader. Many packaged foods harbor hidden sodium. Familiarize yourself with alternative names for sodium, such as monosodium glutamate (MSG) or sodium bicarbonate. Opt for low-sodium or no-added-salt versions of canned goods and condiments to maintain better control over your daily sodium intake.

Fluid Dynamics:

Fluid retention is a common concern for individuals with renal challenges. Be vigilant about your fluid intake, as excess fluids can strain the kidneys. Monitor not only your sodium consumption but also stay mindful of your overall fluid balance.

It's a delicate dance that, when mastered, contributes to maintaining optimal renal function.

Incorporating Healthy Fats

Navigating the Fat Frontier:

Contrary to popular belief, fats are not the enemy; they're essential for overall health. However, the key lies in choosing the right fats. Embrace heart-healthy fats found in avocados, olive oil, and fatty fish. These fats can contribute to a satiated feeling while supporting cardiovascular health — a win-win for your overall well-being.

Mindful Cooking Techniques:

Explore cooking methods that minimize the need for added fats. Slow cooking, the hero of our culinary journey, allows flavors to meld without excessive reliance on oils or butters. Roasting, baking, and grilling are also excellent alternatives that impart delicious flavors without compromising on health.

Portion Prowess:

Even with healthy fats, moderation remains paramount. Be mindful of portion sizes to avoid unnecessary caloric intake. Your body will thank you for providing it with the nourishment it needs without overwhelming it with excess.

Monitoring Protein Intake

Protein Prowess for Renal Health:

Protein is the building block of life, but for those with diabetes and renal concerns, moderation is the key.

Opt for high-quality protein sources such as lean meats, poultry, fish, and plant-based alternatives like legumes and tofu. Distribute your protein intake evenly throughout the day to support muscle function and maintain stable blood sugar levels.

Customizing Protein Portions:

Individualize your protein portions based on your unique dietary needs and renal function. Work closely with your healthcare team to determine the optimal protein intake that aligns with your overall health goals. Remember, moderation is not synonymous with deprivation; it's about finding the right balance for your body.

Protein Partnering with Fiber:

Combine protein-rich foods with high-fiber choices to create well-rounded meals that support digestive health and keep you feeling satisfied. Fiber not only aids in digestion but also helps control blood sugar levels, providing a synergistic effect when paired with lean proteins.

CHAPTER THREE: BREAKFAST DELIGHTS

1. Quinoa and Berry Breakfast Bowl

Servings: 4

Cooking Time: 4 hours on low

Ingredients:

- ✓ 1 cup quinoa, rinsed

- ✓ 2 cups unsweetened almond milk

- ✓ 1 cup mixed berries (blueberries, strawberries)

- ✓ 1 tablespoon chia seeds

- ✓ 1 teaspoon vanilla extract

Preparation:

1. Combine quinoa, almond milk, berries, chia seeds, and vanilla extract in the slow cooker.

2. Cook on low for 4 hours.

3. Serve warm, and garnish with additional berries if desired.

Nutritional Info (per serving): 240 calories, 5g protein, 40g carbohydrates, 6g fiber, 3g fat; Potassium: 220mg, Sodium: 80mg

2. Egg White and Vegetable Frittata

Servings: 6

Cooking Time: 3 hours on low

Ingredients:

- ✓ 2 cups egg whites

- ✓ 1 cup diced bell peppers

- ✓ 1 cup spinach, chopped

- ✓ 1/2 cup low-fat feta cheese

- ✓ Salt and pepper to taste

Preparation:

1. Whisk together egg whites, bell peppers, spinach, feta, salt, and pepper in a bowl.

2. Pour the mixture into the slow cooker.

3. Cook on low for 3 hours or until set.

Nutritional Info (per serving): 120 calories, 15g protein, 6g carbohydrates, 2g fat; Potassium: 180mg, Sodium: 200mg

3. Cinnamon Apple Oatmeal

Servings: 4

Cooking Time: 6 hours on low

Ingredients:

- ✓ 1 cup steel-cut oats

- ✓ 2 apples, peeled and diced

- ✓ 1 teaspoon cinnamon

- ✓ 1/4 cup chopped walnuts

- ✓ 4 cups water

Preparation:

1. Combine oats, apples, cinnamon, walnuts, and water in the slow cooker.

2. Cook on low for 6 hours.

3. Stir well before serving.

Nutritional Info (per serving): 280 calories, 7g protein, 48g carbohydrates, 7g fiber, 8g fat; Potassium: 200mg, Sodium: 5mg

4. Turkey Sausage and Vegetable Casserole

Servings: 6

Cooking Time: 4 hours on low

Ingredients:

- ✓ 1 pound turkey sausage, sliced

- ✓ 1 cup cherry tomatoes, halved

- ✓ 1 cup zucchini, diced

- ✓ 1 cup bell peppers, chopped

- ✓ 8 eggs, beaten

Preparation:

1. Brown the turkey sausage in a skillet.

2. In the slow cooker, layer sausage, tomatoes, zucchini, and bell peppers.

3. Pour beaten eggs over the layers.

4. Cook on low for 4 hours.

Nutritional Info (per serving): 220 calories, 18g protein, 8g carbohydrates, 2g fiber, 12g fat; Potassium: 280mg, Sodium: 350mg

5. Greek Yogurt Parfait

Servings: 4

Prep Time: 10 minutes

Ingredients:

- ✓ 2 cups Greek yogurt

- ✓ 1 cup mixed berries

- ✓ 1/4 cup chopped almonds

- ✓ 1 tablespoon honey

Preparation:

1. In serving glasses, layer Greek yogurt, berries, and almonds.

2. Drizzle honey on top.

3. Refrigerate for at least 1 hour before serving.

Nutritional Info (per serving): 180 calories, 15g protein, 18g carbohydrates, 3g fiber, 6g fat; Potassium: 250mg, Sodium: 50mg

6. Sweet Potato and Spinach Hash

Servings: 4

Cooking Time: 5 hours on low

Ingredients:

- ✓ 2 sweet potatoes, peeled and diced

- ✓ 2 cups fresh spinach

- ✓ 1 onion, chopped

- ✓ 1 teaspoon smoked paprika

- ✓ Salt and pepper to taste

Preparation:

1. Combine sweet potatoes, spinach, onion, paprika, salt, and pepper in the slow cooker.

2. Cook on low for 5 hours.

3. Serve with a poached egg on top if desired.

Nutritional Info (per serving): 160 calories, 4g protein, 36g carbohydrates, 5g fiber, 1g fat; Potassium: 320mg, Sodium: 60mg

7. Salmon and Dill Breakfast Casserole

Servings: 6

Cooking Time: 3 hours on low

Ingredients:

- ✓ 1 can (14 oz) salmon, drained and flaked

- ✓ 1/2 cup chopped fresh dill

- ✓ 1 cup cherry tomatoes, halved

- ✓ 8 eggs, beaten

- ✓ Salt and pepper to taste

Preparation:

1. In a bowl, mix salmon, dill, tomatoes, beaten eggs, salt, and pepper.

2. Pour into the slow cooker.

3. Cook on low for 3 hours or until set.

Nutritional Info (per serving): 230 calories, 20g protein, 6g carbohydrates, 1g fiber, 14g fat; Potassium: 260mg, Sodium: 300mg

8. Chia Seed Pudding with Berries

Servings: 4

Prep Time: 5 minutes

Ingredients:

✓ 1/2 cup chia seeds

✓ 2 cups unsweetened almond milk

✓ 1 teaspoon vanilla extract

✓ 1 cup mixed berries

Preparation:

1. Mix chia seeds, almond milk, and vanilla extract in a bowl.

2. Refrigerate for at least 4 hours or overnight.

3. Serve topped with mixed berries.

Nutritional Info (per serving): 180 calories, 5g protein, 20g carbohydrates, 10g fiber, 9g fat; Potassium: 180mg, Sodium: 70mg

9. Mushroom and Spinach omelet

Servings: 2

Cooking Time: 2 hours on low

Ingredients:

✓ 4 eggs, beaten

✓ 1 cup sliced mushrooms

✓ 1 cup fresh spinach

✓ 1/2 cup shredded low-fat cheese

✓ Salt and pepper to taste

Preparation:

1. Grease the slow cooker with cooking spray.

2. In a bowl, mix eggs, mushrooms, spinach, cheese, salt, and pepper.

3. Pour into the slow cooker and cook on low for 2 hours.

Nutritional Info (per serving): 200 calories, 15g protein, 6g carbohydrates, 2g fiber, 12g fat; Potassium: 240mg, Sodium: 220mg

10. Blueberry Almond Oat Bars

Servings: 8

Cooking Time: 3 hours on low

Ingredients:

- ✓ 2 cups rolled oats

- ✓ 1 cup almond flour

- ✓ 1/2 cup almond butter

- ✓ 1/4 cup honey

- ✓ 1 cup fresh blueberries

Preparation:

1. In a bowl, mix oats, almond flour, almond butter, and honey.

2. Press half of the mixture into the bottom of the slow cooker.

3. Spread blueberries over the oat mixture.

4. Crumble the remaining oat mixture on top.

5. Cook on low for 3 hours.

Nutritional Info (per serving): 250 calories, 8g protein, 30g carbohydrates, 6g fiber, 12g fat; Potassium: 180mg, Sodium: 10mg

CHAPTER FOUR: APPETIZING SOUPS AND STEWS

11. Vegetable and Lentil Soup

Servings: 6

Cooking Time: 4 hours on low

Ingredients:

- ✓ 1 cup dried green lentils, rinsed

- ✓ 4 cups low-sodium vegetable broth

- ✓ 2 carrots, diced

- ✓ 2 celery stalks, chopped

- ✓ 1 onion, finely chopped

Preparation:

1. Combine lentils, vegetable broth, carrots, celery, and onion in the slow cooker.

2. Cook on low for 4 hours.

3. Season with salt and pepper to taste before serving.

Nutritional Info (per serving): 180 calories, 12g protein, 30g carbohydrates, 10g fiber, 1g fat; Potassium: 450mg, Sodium: 150mg

12. Chicken and Vegetable Stew

Servings: 4

Cooking Time: 5 hours on low

Ingredients:

- ✓ 1 pound boneless, skinless chicken thighs, cubed

- ✓ 3 cups low-sodium chicken broth

- ✓ 1 cup carrots, sliced

- ✓ 1 cup green beans, chopped

- ✓ 1 cup potatoes, diced

Preparation:

1. Place chicken, chicken broth, carrots, green beans, and potatoes in the slow cooker.

2. Cook on low for 5 hours.

3. Season with herbs and salt to taste before serving.

Nutritional Info (per serving): 240 calories, 20g protein, 25g carbohydrates, 5g fiber, 6g fat; Potassium: 380mg, Sodium: 180mg

13. Turkey and Quinoa Chili

Servings: 8

Cooking Time: 6 hours on low

Ingredients:

- ✓ 1 pound ground turkey

- ✓ 1 cup quinoa, rinsed

- ✓ 1 can (14 oz) low-sodium diced tomatoes

- ✓ 1 can (14 oz) black beans, drained and rinsed

- ✓ 1 tablespoon chili powder

Preparation:

1. Brown ground turkey in a skillet and drain excess fat.

2. In the slow cooker, combine turkey, quinoa, diced tomatoes, black beans, and chili powder.

3. Cook on low for 6 hours.

Nutritional Info (per serving): 280 calories, 20g protein, 30g carbohydrates, 7g fiber, 9g fat; Potassium: 400mg, Sodium: 200mg

14. Salmon and Vegetable Chowder

Servings: 4

Cooking Time: 3 hours on low

Ingredients:

- ✓ 1 can (14 oz) salmon, drained and flaked

- ✓ 2 cups cauliflower florets

- ✓ 1 cup leeks, sliced

- ✓ 2 cups low-sodium vegetable broth

Preparation:

1. Combine salmon, cauliflower, leeks, and vegetable broth in the slow cooker.

2. Cook on low for 3 hours.

3. Season with dill, salt, and pepper before serving.

Nutritional Info (per serving): 220 calories, 18g protein, 15g carbohydrates, 4g fiber, 10g fat; Potassium: 320mg, Sodium: 180mg

15. Spinach and White Bean Soup

Servings: 6

Cooking Time: 4 hours on low

Ingredients:

- ✓ 2 cans (15 oz each) low-sodium white beans, drained and rinsed

- ✓ 4 cups fresh spinach

- ✓ 1 onion, chopped

- ✓ 3 cloves garlic, minced

- ✓ 4 cups low-sodium vegetable broth

Preparation:

1. In the slow cooker, combine white beans, spinach, onion, garlic, and vegetable broth.

2. Cook on low for 4 hours.

3. Mash some beans for a thicker consistency if desired.

Nutritional Info (per serving): 160 calories, 12g protein, 25g carbohydrates, 8g fiber, 1g fat; Potassium: 350mg, Sodium: 200mg

16. Mushroom and Barley Stew

Servings: 5

Cooking Time: 5 hours on low

Ingredients:

- ✓ 1 cup pearl barley

- ✓ 2 cups mushrooms, sliced

- ✓ 1 onion, finely chopped

- ✓ 3 carrots, diced

- ✓ 4 cups low-sodium vegetable broth

Preparation:

1. Combine barley, mushrooms, onion, carrots, and vegetable broth in the slow cooker.

2. Cook on low for 5 hours.

3. Season with thyme, salt, and pepper before serving.

Nutritional Info (per serving): 200 calories, 8g protein, 40g carbohydrates, 10g fiber, 1g fat; Potassium: 280mg, Sodium: 180mg

17. Tomato Basil Quinoa Soup

Servings: 4

Cooking Time: 4 hours on low

Ingredients:

- ✓ 1 cup quinoa, rinsed

- ✓ 2 cans (28 oz each) low-sodium crushed tomatoes

- ✓ 1 onion, diced

- ✓ 2 cloves garlic, minced

- ✓ 4 cups low-sodium vegetable broth

Preparation:

1. Combine quinoa, crushed tomatoes, onion, garlic, and vegetable broth in the slow cooker.

2. Cook on low for 4 hours.

3. Stir in fresh basil before serving.

Nutritional Info (per serving): 220 calories, 10g protein, 40g carbohydrates, 6g fiber, 2g fat; Potassium: 400mg, Sodium: 150mg

18. Cabbage and Turkey Sausage Soup

Servings: 6

Cooking Time: 3 hours on low

Ingredients:

- ✓ 1 pound turkey sausage, sliced

- ✓ 1/2 head cabbage, shredded

- ✓ 1 onion, chopped

- ✓ 2 cloves garlic, minced

- ✓ 4 cups low-sodium chicken broth

Preparation:

1. Brown turkey sausage in a skillet and drain excess fat.

2. In the slow cooker, combine turkey sausage, cabbage, onion, garlic, and chicken broth.

3. Cook on low for 3 hours.

Nutritional Info (per serving): 180 calories, 15g protein, 20g carbohydrates, 5g fiber, 6g fat; Potassium: 320mg, Sodium: 200mg

19. Broccoli and Cheese Cauliflower Soup

Servings: 4

Cooking Time: 4 hours on low

Ingredients:

- ✓ 2 cups cauliflower florets

- ✓ 2 cups broccoli florets

- ✓ 1 onion, chopped

- ✓ 2 cups low-sodium vegetable broth

- ✓ 1 cup shredded low-fat cheddar cheese

Preparation:

1. Combine cauliflower, broccoli, onion, vegetable broth, and half of the shredded cheese in the slow cooker.

2. Cook on low for 4 hours.

3. Top with the remaining cheese before serving.

Nutritional Info (per serving): 160 calories, 10g protein, 20g carbohydrates, 6g fiber, 5g fat; Potassium: 300mg, Sodium: 180mg

20. Sweet Potato and Black Bean Chili

Servings: 8

Cooking Time: 6 hours on low

Ingredients:

- ✓ 2 sweet potatoes, peeled and diced

- ✓ 2 cans (15 oz each) low-sodium black beans, drained and rinsed

- ✓ 1 can (14 oz) diced tomatoes

- ✓ 1 onion, finely chopped

- ✓ 1 tablespoon chili powder

Preparation:

1. Combine sweet potatoes, black beans, diced tomatoes, onion, and chili powder in the slow cooker.

2. Cook on low for 6 hours.

3. Serve with a dollop of Greek yogurt if desired.

Nutritional Info (per serving): 220 calories, 10g protein, 40g carbohydrates, 8g fiber, 1g fat; Potassium: 350mg, Sodium: 200mg

CHAPTER FIVE: SAVORY MAIN COURSES

21. Balsamic Chicken and Vegetable Medley

Servings: 4

Cooking Time: 4 hours on low

Ingredients:

- ✓ 4 boneless, skinless chicken breasts

- ✓ 1 cup cherry tomatoes, halved

- ✓ 1 zucchini, sliced

- ✓ 1 bell pepper, sliced

- ✓ 1/4 cup balsamic vinegar

Preparation:

1. Place chicken breasts in the slow cooker.

2. Add cherry tomatoes, zucchini, bell pepper, and balsamic vinegar.

3. Cook on low for 4 hours.

4. Serve chicken over a bed of vegetables.

Nutritional Info (per serving): 220 calories, 30g protein, 10g carbohydrates, 3g fiber, 5g fat; Potassium: 380mg, Sodium: 120mg

22. Lemon Garlic Shrimp with Quinoa

Servings: 4

Cooking Time: 2 hours on low

Ingredients:

- ✓ 1 pound shrimp, peeled and deveined

- ✓ 1 cup quinoa, rinsed

- ✓ 2 cloves garlic, minced

- ✓ 1 lemon, juiced

- ✓ 2 cups low-sodium chicken broth

Preparation:

1. Combine shrimp, quinoa, garlic, lemon juice, and chicken broth in the slow cooker.

2. Cook on low for 2 hours.

3. Fluff quinoa before serving with a side of steamed vegetables.

Nutritional Info (per serving): 250 calories, 25g protein, 30g carbohydrates, 4g fiber, 3g fat; Potassium: 320mg, Sodium: 180mg

23. Turkey and Vegetable Stuffed Peppers

Servings: 6

Cooking Time: 4 hours on low

Ingredients:

- ✓ 1 pound ground turkey

- ✓ 6 bell peppers, halved and seeds removed

- ✓ 1 cup quinoa, cooked

- ✓ 1 can (14 oz) low-sodium diced tomatoes

- ✓ 1 teaspoon Italian seasoning

Preparation:

1. Brown ground turkey in a skillet and drain excess fat.

2. In a bowl, mix turkey, quinoa, diced tomatoes, and Italian seasoning.

3. Stuff bell peppers with the mixture and place in the slow cooker.

4. Cook on low for 4 hours.

Nutritional Info (per serving): 230 calories, 20g protein, 25g carbohydrates, 6g fiber, 6g fat; Potassium: 400mg, Sodium: 180mg

24. Mediterranean Eggplant and Chickpea Stew

Servings: 4

Cooking Time: 3 hours on low

Ingredients:

- ✓ 1 large eggplant, diced

- ✓ 1 can (15 oz) chickpeas, drained and rinsed

- ✓ 1 onion, chopped

- ✓ 2 cloves garlic, minced

- ✓ 1 can (14 oz) low-sodium diced tomatoes

Preparation:

1. Combine eggplant, chickpeas, onion, garlic, and diced tomatoes in the slow cooker.

2. Cook on low for 3 hours.

3. Season with oregano, salt, and pepper before serving over quinoa.

Nutritional Info (per serving): 180 calories, 8g protein, 30g carbohydrates, 10g fiber, 3g fat; Potassium: 350mg, Sodium: 120mg

25. Beef and Vegetable Stir-Fry

Servings: 4

Cooking Time: 4 hours on low

Ingredients:

- ✓ 1 pound beef sirloin, thinly sliced

- ✓ 2 cups broccoli florets

- ✓ 1 bell pepper, sliced

- ✓ 1 cup snap peas

- ✓ 1/4 cup low-sodium soy sauce

Preparation:

1. Place beef, broccoli, bell pepper, and snap peas in the slow cooker.

2. Pour soy sauce over the ingredients.

3. Cook on low for 4 hours.

4. Serve over cauliflower rice.

Nutritional Info (per serving): 260 calories, 30g protein, 15g carbohydrates, 6g fiber, 8g fat; Potassium: 400mg, Sodium: 280mg

26. Cilantro Lime Chicken with Brown Rice

Servings: 4

Cooking Time: 3 hours on low

Ingredients:

- ✓ 4 boneless, skinless chicken thighs

- ✓ 1 cup brown rice, cooked

- ✓ 1 bunch cilantro, chopped

- ✓ 2 limes, juiced

- ✓ 1 teaspoon cumin

Preparation:

1. Place chicken thighs in the slow cooker.

2. In a bowl, mix cooked brown rice, cilantro, lime juice, and cumin.

3. Spread the rice mixture over the chicken.

4. Cook on low for 3 hours.

Nutritional Info (per serving): 240 calories, 25g protein, 30g carbohydrates, 4g fiber, 4g fat; Potassium: 320mg, Sodium: 120mg

27. Lemon Herb Tilapia with Spinach

Servings: 4

Cooking Time: 2 hours on low

Ingredients:

- ✓ 4 tilapia fillets

- ✓ 2 cups fresh spinach

- ✓ 1 lemon, sliced

- ✓ 1 teaspoon dried thyme

- ✓ Salt and pepper to taste

Preparation:

1. Place tilapia fillets in the slow cooker.

2. Layer spinach over the fish, then top with lemon slices and thyme.

3. Season with salt and pepper.

4. Cook on low for 2 hours.

Nutritional Info (per serving): 180 calories, 25g protein, 5g carbohydrates, 2g fiber, 6g fat; Potassium: 300mg, Sodium: 120mg

28. Vegetarian Lentil and Mushroom Stew

Servings: 6

Cooking Time: 4 hours on low

Ingredients:

- ✓ 1 cup dried green lentils, rinsed

- ✓ 2 cups mushrooms, sliced

- ✓ 1 onion, chopped

- ✓ 3 carrots, diced

- ✓ 4 cups low-sodium vegetable broth

Preparation:

1. Combine lentils, mushrooms, onion, carrots, and vegetable broth in the slow cooker.

2. Cook on low for 4 hours.

3. Season with rosemary, salt, and pepper before serving.

Nutritional Info (per serving): 220 calories, 15g protein, 30g carbohydrates, 10g fiber, 2g fat; Potassium: 380mg, Sodium: 150mg

29. Spaghetti Squash and Turkey Bolognese

Servings: 4

Cooking Time: 3 hours on low

Ingredients:

- ✓ 1 spaghetti squash, halved and seeds removed

- ✓ 1 pound ground turkey

- ✓ 1 can (14 oz) low-sodium crushed tomatoes

- ✓ 2 cloves garlic, minced

Preparation:

1. Place spaghetti squash halves in the slow cooker.

2. In a skillet, brown ground turkey and add crushed tomatoes and garlic.

3. Spoon turkey mixture over the spaghetti squash.

4. Cook on low for 3 hours.

Nutritional Info (per serving): 250 calories, 20g protein, 25g carbohydrates, 6g fiber, 8g fat; Potassium: 320mg, Sodium: 180mg

30. Chickpea and Vegetable Curry

Servings: 6

Cooking Time: 4 hours on low

Ingredients:

✓ 2 cans (15 oz each) low-sodium chickpeas, drained and rinsed

✓ 2 cups cauliflower florets

✓ 1 bell pepper, chopped

✓ 1 onion, diced

✓ 1 can (14 oz) low-sodium coconut milk

Preparation:

1. Combine chickpeas, cauliflower, bell pepper, onion, and coconut milk in the slow cooker.

2. Cook on low for 4 hours.

3. Season with curry powder, salt, and pepper before serving over brown rice.

Nutritional Info (per serving): 220 calories, 10g protein, 30g carbohydrates, 8g fiber, 6g fat; Potassium: 350mg, Sodium: 180mg

CHAPTER SIX: SIDE DISHES AND ACCOMPANIMENTS

31. Cauliflower and Spinach Mash

Servings: 4

Cooking Time: 3 hours on low

Ingredients:

- ✓ 1 head cauliflower, chopped ,

- ✓ 2 cups fresh spinach

- ✓ 2 cloves garlic, minced

- ✓ 1/4 cup low-sodium vegetable broth

Preparation:

1. Combine cauliflower, spinach, garlic, and vegetable broth in the slow cooker.

2. Cook on low for 3 hours.

3. Mash the mixture until desired consistency.

Nutritional Info (per serving): 80 calories, 5g protein, 15g carbohydrates, 6g fiber, 1g fat; Potassium: 270mg, Sodium: 70mg

32. Herbed Quinoa Pilaf

Servings: 6

Cooking Time: 2 hours on low

Ingredients:

- ✓ 1 cup quinoa, rinsed

- ✓ 2 cups low-sodium vegetable broth

- ✓ 1 onion, finely chopped

- ✓ 1 teaspoon dried thyme

Preparation:

1. Combine quinoa, vegetable broth, onion, and thyme in the slow cooker.

2. Cook on low for 2 hours.

3. Fluff quinoa with a fork before serving.

Nutritional Info (per serving): 150 calories, 5g protein, 25g carbohydrates, 3g fiber, 3g fat; Potassium: 180mg, Sodium: 80mg

33. Garlic and Rosemary Roasted Sweet Potatoes

Servings: 4

Cooking Time: 3 hours on low

Ingredients:

- ✓ 2 large sweet potatoes, peeled and diced

- ✓ 2 cloves garlic, minced

- ✓ 2 tablespoons olive oil

- ✓ 1 teaspoon dried rosemary

Preparation:

1. Toss sweet potatoes, garlic, olive oil, and rosemary in the slow cooker.

2. Cook on low for 3 hours.

3. Stir halfway through the cooking time.

Nutritional Info (per serving): 120 calories, 2g protein, 20g carbohydrates, 4g fiber, 4g fat; Potassium: 280mg, Sodium: 30mg

34. Green Bean Almondine

Servings: 6

Cooking Time: 2 hours on low

Ingredients:

- ✓ 1 pound fresh green beans, trimmed

- ✓ 1/4 cup sliced almonds

- ✓ 2 tablespoons olive oil

- ✓ 1 lemon, juiced

Preparation:

1. Place green beans, sliced almonds, olive oil, and lemon juice in the slow cooker.

2. Cook on low for 2 hours.

3. Toss before serving.

Nutritional Info (per serving): 90 calories, 3g protein, 10g carbohydrates, 4g fiber, 5g fat; Potassium: 200mg, Sodium: 10mg

35. Mushroom and Leek Brown Rice Risotto

Servings: 4

Cooking Time: 3 hours on low

Ingredients:

- ✓ 1 cup brown rice

- ✓ 2 cups mushrooms, sliced

- ✓ 2 leeks, cleaned and chopped

- ✓ 4 cups low-sodium vegetable broth

Preparation:

1. Combine brown rice, mushrooms, leeks, and vegetable broth in the slow cooker.

2. Cook on low for 3 hours.

3. Stir well before serving.

Nutritional Info (per serving): 160 calories, 4g protein, 30g carbohydrates, 5g fiber, 3g fat; Potassium: 240mg, Sodium: 80mg

36. Turmeric and Ginger Carrot Salad

Servings: 4

Cooking Time: 2 hours on low

Ingredients:

- ✓ 1 pound carrots, julienned

- ✓ 1 teaspoon ground turmeric

- ✓ 1 teaspoon fresh ginger, grated

- ✓ 2 tablespoons apple cider vinegar

Preparation:

1. Toss carrots, turmeric, ginger, and apple cider vinegar in the slow cooker.

2. Cook on low for 2 hours.

3. Chill before serving.

Nutritional Info (per serving): 70 calories, 1g protein, 15g carbohydrates, 4g fiber, 0g fat; Potassium: 260mg, Sodium: 60mg

37. Lemon Dill Cucumber Salad

Servings: 4

Cooking Time: 1 hour on low

Ingredients:

- ✓ 2 cucumbers, thinly sliced

- ✓ 1/4 cup fresh dill, chopped

- ✓ 1 lemon, juiced

- ✓ 1 tablespoon olive oil

Preparation:

1. Combine cucumbers, dill, lemon juice, and olive oil in the slow cooker.

2. Toss to coat evenly.

3. Cook on low for 1 hour.

Nutritional Info (per serving): 50 calories, 1g protein, 7g carbohydrates, 2g fiber, 3g fat; Potassium: 200mg, Sodium: 10mg

38. Quinoa and Black Bean Stuffed Bell Peppers

Servings: 6

Cooking Time: 4 hours on low

Ingredients:

- ✓ 6 bell peppers, halved and seeds removed

- ✓ 1 cup quinoa, cooked

- ✓ 1 can (15 oz) low-sodium black beans, drained and rinsed

- ✓ 1 cup corn kernels (fresh or frozen)

Preparation:

1. Stuff bell peppers with a mixture of quinoa, black beans, and corn.

2. Place stuffed peppers in the slow cooker.

3. Cook on low for 4 hours.

Nutritional Info (per serving): 220 calories, 10g protein, 40g carbohydrates, 8g fiber, 2g fat; Potassium: 350mg, Sodium: 80mg

39. Zucchini and Tomato Casserole

Servings: 4

Cooking Time: 3 hours on low

Ingredients:

- ✓ 4 zucchini, sliced

- ✓ 2 tomatoes, sliced

- ✓ 1 onion, thinly sliced

- ✓ 1 teaspoon dried Italian herbs

Preparation:

1. Layer zucchini, tomatoes, and onions in the slow cooker.

2. Sprinkle with dried Italian herbs.

3. Cook on low for 3 hours.

Nutritional Info (per serving): 60 calories, 2g protein, 15g carbohydrates, 4g fiber, 0g fat; Potassium: 320mg, Sodium: 10mg

40. Broccoli and Walnut Salad

Servings: 4

Cooking Time: 2 hours on low

Ingredients:

- ✓ 4 cups broccoli florets

- ✓ 1/2 cup walnuts, chopped

- ✓ 1/4 cup raisins

- ✓ 2 tablespoons balsamic vinegar

Preparation:

1. Combine broccoli, walnuts, raisins, and balsamic vinegar in the slow cooker.

2. Toss to coat evenly.

3. Cook on low for 2 hours.

Nutritional Info (per serving): 120 calories, 5g protein, 15g carbohydrates, 5g fiber, 6g fat; Potassium: 300mg, Sodium: 30mg

CONCLUSION

In concluding this culinary journey through the realms of health and flavor, the "Slow Cooker Diabetic Renal Diet Cookbook" stands as more than just a collection of recipes; it is a testament to the fusion of mindful nutrition and culinary delight. In the tapestry of dietary choices, this cookbook weaves a narrative of empowerment for those navigating the intricate terrain of diabetes and renal concerns.

As we close the lid on this culinary odyssey, let us reflect on the profound impact that conscious eating can have on our overall well-being. The slow cooker, a humble kitchen ally, has emerged as a culinary hero in crafting meals that are not only delicious but also intricately tailored to meet the dietary needs of those grappling with diabetes and renal challenges.

Our journey has taken us through a symphony of flavors, from zesty citrus-infused creations to hearty, protein-packed stews. With each recipe, we have strived not only to tantalize the taste buds but also to nurture the body, recognizing that food is not just sustenance but a powerful tool in managing health.

In a world saturated with culinary options, this cookbook stands out as a beacon of hope for those seeking a harmonious balance between flavor and health. It is a manifesto that declares, with every simmer and sizzle, that a diabetic renal diet need not be a sentence to blandness. Instead, it is an invitation to explore the vibrant palette of ingredients, transforming them into culinary masterpieces that serve as a celebration of life.

We extend our heartfelt gratitude for embarking on this gastronomic expedition with us. May the pages of this cookbook not just be a reference in the kitchen but a source of inspiration and empowerment. As you embark on your own culinary adventures, armed with the knowledge and recipes contained herein, may your meals be a source of nourishment, joy, and a reminder that healthful living need not sacrifice the pleasures of the palate.

In this concluding chapter, let us raise our spoons to a future filled with delectable dishes, thriving health, and the enduring belief that, with the right ingredients and a dash of creativity, a slow cooker can be the catalyst for a journey towards a vibrant and fulfilling life. Cheers to the union of culinary prowess and well-being—may your kitchen continue to be a sanctuary of health, happiness, and savory satisfaction!

BONUS: 30 DAY MEAL PLAN

Day 1:

Breakfast: Slow Cooker Steel-Cut Oats with Berries and Nuts

Lunch: Lentil Soup with Spinach

Dinner: Lemon Garlic Chicken with Roasted Vegetables

Day 2:

Breakfast: Greek Yogurt Parfait with Almonds and Chia Seeds

Lunch: Quinoa and Vegetable Stew

Dinner: Slow Cooker Turkey Chili

Day 3:

Breakfast: Vegetable and Egg Casserole

Lunch: White Bean and Kale Soup

Dinner: Balsamic Glazed Salmon with Sweet Potato

Day 4:

Breakfast: Cottage Cheese Pancakes with Blueberries

Lunch: Chicken and Vegetable Curry

Dinner: Slow Cooker Ratatouille over Brown Rice

Day 5:

Breakfast: Slow Cooker Breakfast Burritos with Whole Wheat Tortillas

Lunch: Minestrone Soup

Dinner: Herb-Crusted Tilapia with Cauliflower Mash

Day 6:

Breakfast: Quinoa Porridge with Cinnamon and Apple

Lunch: Slow Cooker Black Bean Soup

Dinner: Teriyaki Chicken with Broccoli and Brown Rice

Day 7:

Breakfast: omelet with Spinach, Tomatoes, and Feta

Lunch: Split Pea Soup with Ham

Dinner: Mediterranean Vegetable and Chickpea Stew

Day 8:

Breakfast: Overnight Chia Seed Pudding with Mixed Berries

Lunch: Turkey and Vegetable Chili

Dinner: Lemon Herb Shrimp with Asparagus

Day 9:

Breakfast: Whole Grain Toast with Avocado and Poached Egg

Lunch: Red Lentil and Vegetable Curry

Dinner: Slow Cooker Beef and Vegetable Stew

Day 10:

Breakfast: Berry Smoothie with Greek Yogurt

Lunch: Chicken and Quinoa Soup

Dinner: Garlic Rosemary Pork Tenderloin with Roasted Brussels Sprouts

Day 11:

Breakfast: Spinach and Mushroom Frittata

Lunch: Slow Cooker Cauliflower and Chickpea Curry

Dinner: Herb-Marinated Grilled Chicken with Quinoa Salad

Day 12:

Breakfast: Almond Butter and Banana Smoothie

Lunch: Vegetable and Barley Soup

Dinner: Slow Cooker Lemon Herb Cod with Zucchini Noodles

Day 13:

Breakfast: Apple Cinnamon Quinoa Bowl

Lunch: Lentil and Vegetable Stew

Dinner: Turkey and Sweet Potato Slow Cooker Casserole

Day 14:

Breakfast: Scrambled Eggs with Tomatoes and Peppers

Lunch: Slow Cooker Black-Eyed Pea Soup

Dinner: Grilled Salmon with Dill Sauce and Roasted Brussels Sprouts

Day 15:

Breakfast: Overnight Oats with Chopped Walnuts and Berries

Lunch: Chicken and Brown Rice Soup

Dinner: Slow Cooker Vegetable Lasagna

Day 16:

Breakfast: Whole Wheat Pancakes with Sugar-Free Syrup

Lunch: Quinoa Salad with Chickpeas and Veggies

Dinner: Lemon Garlic Shrimp with Quinoa

Day 17:

Breakfast: Avocado and Tomato Toast on Whole Grain Bread

Lunch: Spinach and White Bean Soup

Dinner: Slow Cooker Chicken Cacciatore with Cauliflower Rice

Day 18:

Breakfast: Greek Yogurt with Sliced Peaches and Almonds

Lunch: Minced Turkey and Vegetable Stew

Dinner: Baked Cod with Herbed Quinoa

Day 19:

Breakfast: Blueberry Chia Seed Pudding

Lunch: Slow Cooker Lentil and Kale Stew

Dinner: Turkey Meatballs in Marinara Sauce with Zucchini Noodles

Day 20:

Breakfast: Veggie and Cheese omelet

Lunch: Red Lentil and Spinach Soup

Dinner: Slow Cooker Garlic Herb Chicken with Mashed Cauliflower

Day 21:

Breakfast: Banana Walnut Smoothie with Greek Yogurt

Lunch: Slow Cooker Quinoa and Vegetable Stew

Dinner: Grilled Chicken with Lemon Basil Quinoa

Day 22:

Breakfast: Spinach and Feta Egg Muffins

Lunch: Chickpea and Tomato Curry

Dinner: Slow Cooker Turkey and Vegetable Casserole

Day 23:

Breakfast: Overnight Chia Pudding with Kiwi and Pomegranate Seeds

Lunch: Black Bean and Vegetable Soup

Dinner: Baked Cod with Tomato and Olive Relish

Day 24:

Breakfast: Almond Flour Pancakes with Fresh Berries

Lunch: Lentil and Sweet Potato Stew

Dinner: Slow Cooker Lemon Garlic Shrimp with Cauliflower Rice

Day 25:

Breakfast: Greek Yogurt Parfait with Granola and Mango

Lunch: Chicken and Barley Soup

Dinner: Herb-Roasted Pork Loin with Steamed Green Beans

Day 26:

Breakfast: Avocado and Berry Smoothie Bowl

Lunch: Slow Cooker Quinoa Chili

Dinner: Teriyaki Salmon with Stir-Fried Broccoli and Brown Rice

Day 27:

Breakfast: Vegetable and Cheese omelet with Whole Grain Toast

Lunch: Red Lentil and Vegetable Curry

Dinner: Slow Cooker Chicken and Mushroom Casserole

Day 28:

Breakfast: Apple Cinnamon Oatmeal

Lunch: Spinach and White Bean Minestrone Soup

Dinner: Grilled Tilapia with Lemon Dill Sauce and Roasted Brussels Sprouts

Day 29:

Breakfast: Quinoa Porridge with Mixed Berries

Lunch: Slow Cooker Black Bean and Vegetable Stew

Dinner: Turkey and Vegetable Stir-Fry with Quinoa

Day 30:

Breakfast: Scrambled Eggs with Spinach and Tomatoes

Lunch: Lentil and Brown Rice Soup

Dinner: Slow Cooker Balsamic Chicken with Roasted Vegetables

Made in the USA
Las Vegas, NV
11 December 2024